# BEAMS OF LIGHT

Scarlett Ellson

Bent Key Publishing

ISBN: 978-1-915320-09-4

Bent Key Publishing
Owley Wood Road, Weaverham
bentkeypublishing.co.uk

Edited by Rebecca Kenny @ Bent Key
Cover art © Samantha Sanderson-Marshall @ SMASH Design and Illustration
smashdesigns.co.uk

Printed in the UK by Mixam Ltd.

*To us; all of the people that couldn't see a future — but now can.*

# CONTENTS

# BEAMS OF LIGHT

# TIME

My heart is heavy,
These broken fingers bleed out,
Time is a sad thing.

# WHITE

A white noise compilation
Like shards of glass, whistling along the pavement.
And our skin:
The screaming laugh of ecstasy — or the absence of it. It is gone.
A neon sign, raging: ABANDONMENT.
An argument of chipped teeth, broken mouths and then: nothing.
Just a whisper of a memory of a memory of a memory
of a memory of them.
The breaking of all of the bones in our fingers
until they reflect our hearts.
A magnitude of splinters, compiled here in a Christmas card,
Ready to *starry-night-holy-night* to the ground when opened.
Dirty-knuckled, sweaty-browed,
Wrists singing and then stinging from past-life slices.
These ambient, audible sounds are absent;
No lyrical humming, no audience exclaiming;
It's like dreaming sweetly while the rest of the world moves on.

Being adored is the best thing you can be until you know better.

Until then, it's like bubbles in a wine glass slowly going still.
You can't hear love scream when you cut it open
with a sharp fingernail,
But you can feel its vocal cords rattle with it,
Can watch it dance in the reflection of a mirror, reflected in the
glass of a window,
Stare at its silent lips as its gums bleed
and drown out the pounding.
A silent movie. Palms thrown back on foreheads and
The wringing of hands until it comes back to this:

**Every single thing is just white noise.**

A shy, tepid thing that doesn't draw attention to itself
But instead shakes and folds into a soundless monotone.
A destiny that our broken jaws cannot
sound out loud enough for the deaf hearts.

But for now,
At least we have something other than *white*.

# W H O  Λ M  I ?

Will I always be ripped open; bleeding raw
With salt in every single sore?
Is this all there is?
Or is there more?
And if there is, then —
What's it for?

# EGO - SCHMEGO

They call me ego boost;
They call me warm —
Say: *I feel better now.*
Say — nothing.

They wash their hands in my light,
Quench their thirst in my pool,
Find their shoes —
And go
    go
      go

Show me their scars,
Their heart,
Their art.
Scream: ***MAKE ME FEEL GOOD***.

    And I do

        And they go

They call me ego boost.

        And that's all that I am.

# L I G H T

Is that the light or
Am I hallucinating?
I am reaching out.

# SENSORY OVERLOAD

Okay, it's the day's end / take off your shoes at the door / rub sore ankles / sigh heavily / take off the weighted jacket of the day / leave it on the floor / set the house alarm / omit no zones / hear it *beep, beep, beep* as it notices your presence / wait forty-five seconds before it starts going off / let it keep going off / pass through to the living room / turn on the TV / let it play static / take out your moon-shaped earrings / toss them on a nesting table / unpin your hair and shake it loose / drop the pin as you make your way to the kitchen / in the kitchen turn on the blender / ask Alexa to play HARD HOUSE TRANCE / turn on the coffee machine / put the empty washing machine on / take off your bra / throw it behind you / turn both taps on / leave them on / even after the sink starts to overflow / put the empty dryer on the longest cycle / enter the bathroom / pull off your fake eyelashes / discard them / don't look where they land or what they stick to / turn the bath taps on full / turn your electric toothbrush on / the electric razor too / leave them both rattling in the sink / wipe your eye makeup down your face with a warm towelette / turn on the shower / flush the toilet / open the window / sigh again / leave the bathroom / connect to Bluetooth speaker / play Death Metal / take off your fake smile / take off your bracelets / hear them clang as they drop to the floor / wipe your lipstick off on the bottom of your t-shirt / boil the kettle / turn the microwave on full / ask Alexa to turn the volume up / put the computer on / blast 80s Hits / feel your head pound with the beginnings of a headache / take off your trousers / turn up the static on the living room TV / boil the kettle again / make a cup of tea / sit on sofa / sigh again / **relax** / **relax** / **RELAX.**

# LOVE ME, LOVE ME, LOVE ME

My body is always begging to be loved. Just once. Finally.
Especially after I've starved it and carved it,
And left pieces of it in jars. It's
Hard for these moments of hatred to pass,
And so I cast my mind back to when I was thirteen,
Drawing razor blades along my skin, just to feel something.
To make a hole, cause an opening,
Just somewhere to let the fucking light in.

And now, at twenty-four,
I could slash a razor blade across my throat and be done with this,
But it's impossible to do that. So instead
I sew daisies into the open wounds of my wrists.
They make pretty bracelets — if you can get past the blood.

Which most people can't

And that's okay, because they didn't ask for this,
Nor did I — but it kind-of happened, like a chemical and catalyst,
You add depression and loneliness to anxiety
And then you're standing on the precipice of ending this.

I don't want to be remembered as a forgery. A phoney.
Someone that pretended.
But there are so many versions of me out there and I
Can't live up to every single one of them:
And I have pretended.

Growing up, that's what they told me to do,
*Just pretend to be happy and you will be!* But don't they see?

I've tried to.
I've been happy for fourteen years now, sadly—
And honestly? Happiness isn't all it's cracked up to be.
But anyway I digress.
I just want to. Be. Loved.
~~Oh, those pretty daisies.~~

# HURT IS A FAMILIAR PLACE

My heart is an antique clock.
It rings out my pain every hour, on the hour —
Waking me from my sizzling slumber;
It hears me peel myself from the sticky sheets,
The sunrise laughing maniacally at my sodden cheeks.
The sky is like a colourful pill I dispense
For my darling broken heart.
Golden Hour brings you up;
Blue Hour brings you right back down.
And by night time, my knuckles drag along the corridor,
Leaving smears of him
and me and you and them and her and us —
There are some pieces of me that just never get returned.
So I'm standing in the window, just waiting to catch fire:
If I could just get to blue, maybe I'll begin to melt away.
Instead I'm tip-toeing across every crack
in these splintered floorboards,
Trying to find the **moon** between
where the windowsill meets the wall:
I swear it, friends; I've been here before.
And I can't stop thinking about it.

# LONELY SOUL SONG

Loneliness is stocked up in the fridge again —
It's behind the mayonnaise and the rotting cucumber
Waiting to be spread on my toast in the morning;
Tiny flecks of it are sprinkled with the sugar —
Ready for two teaspoons mixed with my morning coffee;
Ready to go down the hatch and sit in the hollow of my heart.

It's behind the tins of tomato soup that everyone swears they love
(but nobody eats,)
It's under the sink with the chemicals and the bin bags,
It's in the bathroom cabinet, hugging my toothbrush,
It's in the underwire of my bra.
It's stuck in the gaps in my teeth that I never got braces for;
It grazes my sensitive gums raw.
I step on it as I force my feet into the shoes that almost still fit me,
It nicks my foot and I very nearly don't notice it

Until I do.

And then it's sweeping the hair off of my face,
And saying my name in the most romantic of ways,
And I want it to stay,

Let it sit with its tiny claws hooked into my collarbones,
Scraping and aching —
Whispering in a language of sadness
Only I understand.

# SUN

Winter-chilled breathing,
The sun is shining bright now,
Please just grab my hand.

# SHAPE-SHIFTER

I am a shapeshifter.
I keep pirouetting towards resolution and stop
Just at the edge to run my fingers along it.
The dust looks like honey glaze on my fingertips
But when I put them to my lips,
It tastes like the broken heart of sorrow all over again.

This world is a canyon I cannot resist falling into;
Even though it hurts me,
Even though I was born from another one.
When I close my eyes, I sometimes dream my skin ripples
Into that of a lion's and I'm eating my own insides:
I am so blood-red-slathered in the filthy stain of nicotine yellow.
I try to make it into something beautiful, like a sunset,
Unify them until they mimic the warmth of apricots,
But the colours look rotten and perplexed.

So I shift again and call everything about me a sunflower
And I just keep adding yellow until I can't breathe;
Talk myself into it and then out of it again
Until I am bursting out of my comfort like confetti.
And just like that, I'm a complicated thing
Hanging out the window
As the streetlights pass by, hopeful and fleeting.
Roaring under tunnels while the entire universe fails to speak.
How long will it be before I shift again?

# TEMPORARY SOMETHING

I am going backwards      — to before,

My thoughts about you faltering, friend.

You are different somehow,
Maybe I am too.

Maybe that's just how people drift,

How we grow into something                    so different to
what we are known as.

Maybe that's how people end up becoming        u n d o n e,
  and

A    P    A    R    T    .

S e p a r a t e .

Incompatible for one another now,

                                        So you are different, friend.

Maybe I grew West,

                                                And you
                                         grew East,



Maybe we just do not fit together anymore.


*F r i e n d .*

# LIFE IS A FUNNY THING; ARE YOU LAUGHING?

Sweet angels don't sing here anymore
and all I need is a night's lullaby.
If I could hear the way the clocks wind the hands of time all
around the world, then maybe I could stop time itself at this
moment. But to feel what exactly? To feel *safe*.
Instead, I've been buying cakes by the dozen just to fill this
empty hollow shade of grey inside of my stomach.
Friend, this is not really about feeling hungry.
If I were an animal I'd be something you hit
with your car before you kept going.
(This is simply an anecdote for my headless hollow heart)
Please don't even stop long enough to examine the damage
or identify the species;
I'm not good enough to strap me to your roof
to take home and devour.
I couldn't last you the winter if I tried.

Shake me from your pockets like loose change and watch me fall
dispassionately to the ground instead.
I can clitter-clatter with bareness and you can hear it too
if you put your ear to the ground.
Maybe this is a heartbreak song,
Maybe I've been breaking up with myself for one hundred years
Just over and over and over again
And yet I come home and find myself on the sofa.
Did I forget to evict myself again?
Did these lonely hands find my throat instead of my heart
and just claw, claw, claw..?
Am I just chewing on ice cubes to take away the pain?

Or am I lost in the kitchen listening to the microwave ping —
like its abrupt high pitch could slice me away from here
and leave me puddled on the sunny kitchen tiles.
Will I feel the sizzle on my skin as I slip away?
I am researching how to exist among myself and coming up with
*no results found* and oh how hilarious that is.

Ha ha ha ha ha h**a ha ha ha ha ha**.

# GLITTER

Glitter with me here,
I am not afraid of it;
I am whole and happy.

# HAPPINESS

Happiness kissed me on the forehead this morning,
Opened the window to the fresh morning dew
And left out of the front door with its head held high.
It didn't make me breakfast; I'd have asked for an omelette or a
frittata or that bougie thing you can get for brunch in most
restaurants — something with avocado.
It didn't leave a note to say where it had gone or if it was coming
back. My eyes opened to nothingness and its lasting scent
on the breeze through the window,
I rolled over to find an aching emptiness sleeping gently next to me
instead. Snoring in vowels.
My body was numb enough to hurt but I didn't cry;
I told myself to get up but couldn't seem to.
A wash of citrus rushes through me — stinging yellow.
The taste of last night's love is still on my tongue; the ceiling
looked like a storm I didn't have the energy to fight again.
Open clouds of perfect silver rushed in and poured down
and I welcomed it open-mouthed, eyelashes fluttering
and with rosy-cheeked solace.

It takes me eight whole days to get out of bed;
I don't brush my teeth for four.
I eat nothing but Cheese Strings and
sing sad songs to the plants for twelve.
It takes me almost nineteen whole days to realise
that it will come back
because it cannot resist me.

# THE STORY OF THE ADDICT, THE WRITER AND THE FAMILY

More often than sometimes, I can pretend like it isn't happening
But sometimes, I wish I could write you out of this cataclysm
you've found yourself in;
Actively put yourself at the epicentre for so long, now.

I could write it all into fiction with a pen I bought from *Waterstones*
for a very unreasonable price;
Scratch away the bad parts with fountain-pen ink from *WH Smith*,
Cross it all out with a red ballpoint pen —
like all my favourite teachers did to my poetry and stories.
It made me a better writer. So do you think that I could
make this better with a pen and a sheet of paper?
With some good ol' fashioned determination?
I could write you some kickass sidekicks that have special gifts
and fight beside you (or for you) recklessly.

I could write the drugs into dragons and we could all fight them
with our bare hands or our knives and swords — or our fangs.
I could write up some mountains for us to climb as a metaphor
but when we reach the top, holy *shit* won't it be incredible though?
I could write our Mother's tears away
And fix our Father's heart
And stop our Brother's anxiety
from almost a thousand miles away.
I could give your daughter her mum back.
I could, I could do it: but I am just one person
and words are the only weapon that I have.
The addict will still be an addict,
The dragons won't really exist,
And the mountains will be there because mountains are real
but we wouldn't be climbing them.

It would still be me sitting here, daydreaming about writing
another problem I can't control into fiction.
So for now, we will all just go on with the hurt.
Mother's tears will still fall,
Father's heart will still break,
Brother still won't know what to do;
Your daughter still won't have her mum.
And me?

Well, more often than sometimes I can pretend
like it's not happening...
But sometimes I'm so highly aware that I can't write it away
or make it okay.

# IGNORING MY INTUITION
# UNTIL IT NEARLY KILLS ME

Hey, do you feel that? The air is alive and my veins are humming. When it gets like this everything is so loud and foreign and I don't know where I am. In the tiny hours when nothing happens; I know something is about to. I don't know how I know this, let's call it a feeling. What else is there to call it? Yet it is more than that — it's knowing something is about to happen but not knowing when.

That anticipation sits quietly with fizz, floating atop the acid in my stomach. Electricity reaches the Earth from each nerve ending I am holding on to for safe keeping. It builds, gigantic, in my heart until it is clanging against the vibrations... or along with them. Bile rises high and sharp and burning because it feels like power and yet the complete absence of it. I do not control the way the universe interacts with my place-holder made of skin. Instead, I have to take a minute to remember what breathing consists of as tiny beads of perspiration exit and then fall.

Falling would be a good way to describe it. Do you feel it too? Like every single thing that makes the body work is on fire but with lightning and it's digging up every single skin cell of mine one by one to get a little bit further under me. I'm so charged I can hear the electricity in the sockets singing back. Like *welcome to this higher level... we've been waiting for you.*

And when it stops and it's gone, everything goes quiet like that moment at a funeral before the gospel choir begins to sing. You're left all-knowing and unknown and yet you are sat with a box in your lap full of emotions.

That you have to untangle —
And sort through —

And you're empty.

*What was that?*

I could put it down to the anxiety of my dreams chasing me from sleep and what if it is? What if it's my unconscious thoughts telling me what I already know. *I'M SCARED.*

I could put it down to the wind, its rumbling growls of simple destruction shaking me from sleep. But if I did that then I'd just be continuing the pattern: we've been ignoring this for years.

And having said all of this, the creeping sun gnaws at the silk of my essence. Dawn is breaking like a fragile, desolate thing. And so I carry on with my day — I forget the message after two. Pick up right where I left off — that spark inside of me quieted by mundane things like the sound of the dryer or the rumble of the wheels of the bins being dragged to the curb.

And I continue like nothing happened, like this existence was made from foil and Sellotape and thrown in the printer to copy one-hundred-thousand times. Being ignorant is never the hard part; it's just a consequence of existing: a present wrapped in fragile tissue paper and then taken away before Christmas.

These are the things they teach us not to notice and I've been noticing and ignoring them sporadically for years. It's easier that way, really. Like I can't catch myself falling if I can't see it happening before it happens.

So the day starts and everything goes back to normal.

*For God's sake; tell me you felt it too?*

# A CELEBRATION OF LOVE

We twirl around one another;
Heartbeats one. Electricity.
They say sparks fly but for us, everything surged;
We could've set the whole damn universe on fire.
Cold park benches, roundabout pavements,
Desperados.
We could've run away but oh!
What a joy it was to be seen.
*I love you* said drunkenly and too early,
Falling asleep on pavements
Before you could make it all the way home.
We breathed in each other's darkness,
Tried to warm it between our palms; held it up to the moon
To see if we could get it to glow green.
Smoking cigarettes, sharing anecdotes;
The common ground we trod upon became so beautiful as we
Planted our roots deep within each other's bodies,
Came up for air, briefly;
Found the sun somewhere and stepped out into it,
Watered ourselves and one another;
Watched our leaves flourish,
Our roots deepen.
Found ourselves growing together;
Finding, trying.
Planting the seed.
After we came back to reality —
Found a floor to lay it on —
Spent time being patient,
Found a river to reside by —

Pressed our palms to the Earth —
Felt lucky. Felt human.
Drank my coffee decaf and my alcohol zero;
Danced in the kitchen by the under-counter lights
And the colourful lamp.
Shopped for the perfect rug;
Home. Safe.
Had no TV
And spent our time delving even further
Into the beauty of our love.
Tried harder;
Loved like we were set alight and burning,
Like it was our last chance to before the end;
Coffee at the kitchen table in the morning sun,
Conversations and art.
Found out that all along, we were our own demons;
Laid them to bed with their edges blunted,
Sang sweetly in the bedroom;
Giggled softly between each gasp —
Oh, how love makes you explode when it's right!
We still twirl around one another,
Heartbeats one. Electricity.
And oh, how I never want that connection to

                                        trip out.

# GIVE ME IT

Cross my heart and hope:
Life is a beautiful thing
And I want it, please.

# MOON MAGICK

It's a full moon.
How my hands shake,
How they reach up to the sombre skies,
I try to catch the stars in my palms and hold,

Hold on tight.

These galaxies are swirling worlds of potential
And I wouldn't mind a taste.
Sometimes expanding is just another word for letting go
which feels like dying but
I've listened intently to the way that luminous sky tells me
it's okay...
To how the moon sits so sweetly
in her blush leather armchair, praying.

What if I have more power than I realise?
What if I have less than I wish?

Have you felt the moon's kiss recently?
Have you stopped looking out at night and wondering
if any of this is meant for you?
I hope you have.
I hope you've noticed how the ocean kisses each toe,
Morphs itself into precious fingers
To show you this world has been holding you
lovingly
this whole time.

I think we're going to be okay.

# LET IT GO

Let it go
Like leaves blown by the wind —
Here in circles, floating, and then gone.

Tell yourself you'll scream,
Gather up your strength, tip your head back and rage at the sun
in a burst of fiery anguish
But when the screaming stops and your throat is filled with blood,
        You'll be okay.

Tell yourself it's okay to find yourself rummaging through ashes
of all the things you thought you'd turned your back on and
burned to the ground.

Tell yourself it's the idea of not worrying that makes you claw
at yourself with split and broken fingernails,
That if this was a gun instead of a mountain to climb, you'd have
gotten out of bed a little easier.

Tell yourself if you want to hide in the smallest box you can find,
Use some tools to tinker the inner parts of yourself and
Rearrange until everything feels — just right.
        That's okay too.

Do all of those things,

        Let yourself rattle with emotion

        Detonate with feeling
        But then give yourself permission to

                                Let it go.

# LET'S NOT CALL IT HEALING

Let's not call it healing:
Let's call it that thing we did and then undid and melted into;
Let's call it that thing that took an inch off of our dizzying grace.
Let's call it the times we've sieved the salt out of the sea
Just to compliment the sweetness;
Let's call it the times we've sat in the tormented silence,
With neither hands nor luscious heartbeat
And then found ourselves
Known inside.
Let's call it the times we built the palm trees up from the ground
With our bare hands only for the frost to come
And kill everything that was alive;
Let's call it that thing we did in the reminiscence
Of morose existence;
The thing that banged our bodies against sharp rocks
To crack us open, drink those glorious juices
And leave the flesh behind.
Let's call it *that thing* that only drew us back
To propel us forth again;
Let's call it that thing we will continue to keep trying,
That thing that is always returning, always waiting to be found.
Always ready for us.
Let's not call it healing.
Let's call it that thing that zig zags between broken and mended
Before finally settling on *happy to exist.*

Earth lay flat, silky moon lover — and then expand with each sequence of breath: *inhale, exhale.* My chest rises in purple slithers of life; the birds lay upside-down in their nests and the raindrops refracted and coalesced on the ground into a flooded swamp. The children went away today and now all the adults are all making love with each other. Chew valerian root; let it soothe like a thousand-year-long sleep and wake to mountains forming like friendly giants wearing docile flat caps. Hop from vinyl record to vinyl record and cannon-ball into the furry lake; feel yourself drip decadently through the bottom of the earth. Pass through each season in slow motion; watch the leaves grow backwards into non-existence; watch them grow forwards onto the rocks. Listen to the trees wake up and crack all of their joints; hear them take a breath in, begin to respire again. *Inhale, exhale.* See mirrors reflect the ground in the sky so everything continues, forever. Follow the cobblestones to your soul's chest, open it up, whisper *it's okay;* let your tears trickle along your wrists, open up heart-shaped secrets and sprinkle them into the air. Watch them pop like fireworks, one huge bang after another; create a new world, lick it wide-open and pant. *Inhale, exhale.* Watch it curve and arch and transcend. Everything is waking up; places inside chest cavities peep their eyes open. It holds its magic in the rocks; it holds the magic close to its chest and everything smiles and yawns. Taste the sugar pathway on the ground; it swirls with lustre towards the brush. Find the hills of rolling peridot; see them kaleidoscope in swishing circles; lay your body down — the sun blinking. Nodding. Knowing. Feel your tippy-toes tingle; buzz upwards with a fuzz of grace, feel feverish as your heart starts to calm, encompassed in melted gold and salacious glitter. Find the Milky Way; tie a string around its ethereal concept and keep it in your pocket in case you ever need to levitate. Let the moonbeams shine lavender on your iridescent skin. Everything is temporary and the future is just a game of who can pretend the longest.

# SWEET CHILD OF SUMMER

Heat of summer sun,
Hope in the shape of weather:
It's okay; it's okay.

# STAY GOLDEN

*After Olivia Bella*

This place here: it's a knife's edge,
A place to stay *en pointe* and gosh! Don't fall!
Her heartbeat of a hummingbird's wings, woodpecker soul,
Passer of humble silence and then
A smattering of real life.
Reality doesn't quite have the same candescence as pretend;
It doesn't twirl around your finger in a weave of excellence.
Reality is her imagination's vignette,
She can ignore it if she really concentrates on the centre parts.
But how long until somebody claps their hands
And she can't deny that this is where she truly exists,
No matter how many times she clicks her heels?
Sometimes, she has to remind herself of all
Of the gorgeous things of this existence,
That her fluttering heartbeat sat forgotten in her chest is purpose,
That her sanguine soul is always searching for promise,
And sometimes she has to remind herself
That she is the only one that makes it.

There is no consequence to loving herself.

So scream aloud, darling;
I can hear the volley of her heart echo and then deplete
I tell her, *please don't dwindle, darling —*
*You are shining gold.*

# REMEMBER ME

Remember her lips when you taste mine.
Remember cold roof tiles on our aching backs,
Remember praying to God in June that
December wouldn't kill you.
Remember seasons changing, white kissing green —
Melting honey yellow and back again.
Remember loving so hard it makes your heart feel like needles;
Remember numb fingers and toes and the way that they burn
The closer you get them to the fire.
Remember seven-PM relaxing and four-AM romanticising of life,
Remember doing the best that you can.
Remember drinking a coffee before it's gone cold.
When it's hot enough to burn.
Remember me when your lips press against your favourite mug;
Remember how I chose it because it was my favourite mug too.
Remember that I used to put my lips in the exact same spot
As I drank my morning coffee.
Please remember me.
Remember I loved you before I could even put into words
What love was,
Before Eve bit into the apple and before the snake hissed.
Before Adam's rib,
Before the Garden of Eden.
Please remember I loved you before my mouth could even
Make its own sounds.
Before cavemen, before the dinosaurs, before the Big Bang.
I loved you back when it wasn't even easy to.
So please remember me if you can.

# UNTITLED

We are dancing in the rain.
No, wait — sorry, we are dancing in our dreams,
And it's not raining; it's lightning and we
Are effervescent with thunder.
Everything is green and furry and smells like summer sun.
We find our homes in the back of hollowed out trees,
Grow basil from our fingertips and our separated wrists.
There are spiders in our hair and we laugh at each and every leg.
Here, the air is light and as we breathe gently bubbles appear.
The trees speak to us in their own silky language and
We understand.
They reach for us with feather fingertips and curtsey.
We bow back.
The clouds turn ivory and then pink in a vivacious song and dance;
We leak hidden energy from our veins to the earth and it is
Returned in a shimmering of light.
We awake to purples and blues and the sound of water
Kissing rock,
Walk barefoot with gentle feet, place glittering stones around us
In the shape of hearts.
We watch the waterfalls surge gracefully into rockpools, dunk our
Toes in, then our thighs, then our souls.
Feel the water cleanse — charge — create.
Deep dive beneath the surface and feel engulfed, cuddled —
Remembered.
Realise that we can breathe underneath it. Find a hole made from
seaweed at the depths, we pull and pull and pull —
Open a gap we can fit our fingers through, then our wrists, then
Our hearts.
Catapult further into untethered existence — feel flowery wings
Sprout and bud and grow. Levitate and then soar above
Everything, let it make us feel tiny. Let it make us feel free.

Float there in the second of silence before the animals chime
In unison.
We are filled with the opulence of joy,
So uncomplicated and weightless.

It coats our skin and our scars with opal shimmer; as the sun
Catches us we sparkle every colour on the spectrum.
And we are present, and free, and we're inviting you to come too.

All of this leads to a new world — a better one.

# DEAR FRIEND

Dear Friend —
I hope you've found some happiness
In the sodden, soggy bottom of your despair;
I hope you've been ticking off the days with yellow ochre paint.
Or magenta.
That after I've sent this out to you, I don't find out that you drown
in the core of your tears — on some sad empty Tuesday
when the sky was growling.
That you haven't slowly emptied yourself through the hairline
cracks in your cup —

Dear Friend —
I hope I didn't miss you steadily spilling away;
That, I'd have at least noticed.
And knowing how knees knock, I would've been able to find a way
to patch up the damage,
Melt gold into the tiny gaps of your grief and
Pour and pour until you're somehow full once again.

Dear Friend —
Instead, I wish you rolling hills of the richest green
and late nights in the comfiest armchairs with big blankets;
I hope you're patient enough to wait for the fireflies
to come to you,
And even when you're not, I hope you find a way to mix and
make your own source of light.

I hope you feel the buzzing inside of your wondrous body sizzle to
a stop so final that you explain to the rest of us how peace feels.
Like the ocean, I hope you decide to kiss everybody that dares to
come close to you.

Dear Friend —
I hope that inside every smear of grey you can find a smash of

**Colour**

And at the end of it all,
You can sit in the centre of the Earth with a cup of tea,
And smile.
And mean it.

# HOW SHINY NEW WE ARE

We learn to breathe.
We stand and watch the plants in the yard bloom;
We don't avoid telling stories about the monsters under the bed.
They pay rent now.
We dabble in the creative arts, sew the holes in our jeans,
Knit jumpers with three arms in Baltic blue;
We do not complain.
Form our hands into thank-yous;
We do our best
Wrap tinsel around ourselves on the dark days,
Brew tea all afternoon.
Leave the knives in the drawer where they belong.
We smile.
We try.
We are healing.

# H E ∧ L

We made it, my love.
We are gentle and free and
We are made again.

# ACKNOWLEDGEMENTS

How is it possible for me — a poet, a writer, a lover of words — to describe how phenomenal this is..? I don't even know where to start.

Thank you to the one and only Rebecca Kenny for making this possible in the first place. The first time I ever performed poetry was at your book launch; you've introduced me to so many supportive and incredibly talented poets and made the poetry community feel like home for me.

Thank you to all of the poets that I have met and that have inspired me endlessly, cheered me on, supported me, believed in me and have been so kind: Areeba, Olivia, Caitlin, Dorian, Meagan, Sara Catherine, Malgosia, Kamakshi, Jen, Ant, and so many others.

Thank you to Claire, the OG of my writer friends and the person who introduced me to haiku; she has always inspired me with anything she writes and has always supported anything I've written.

Thank you to Graham, who has not only been the light in my life but has repeatedly made me realise that I'm my own light, too. I love you. The way you see the world amazes me every day, as do you. Thank you for listening to me talk poetry without ever telling me to shut up.

And to you, reading this right now, if you've got this far and are still reading, thank you. I hope this little book of poetry has given you something, even just a small sense that you are not alone. When we open our hearts and share with honesty and good intentions, there's a chain reaction among everybody that always ends in love.

Thank you everybody for being part of my chain reaction in some way.

I also want to give a special shout out to Stevie, Caitlin, and Eddie. It's an honour to be published alongside such unbelievable talent.

Love, Scar x

# ABOUT THE AUTHOR

scarlett Ellson is a bisexual poet from Hessle in the North-East of England. She lives on the coast with her partner and two daughters and works full-time in public service. She has been writing since she was a child, and sharing her poetry since 2020.

Her work has its footing in human nature, the spiritual realm, the idea of solitude and loneliness and the connections we make in our lives; this is influenced by her interest in spirituality and wellbeing. She is seen by her peers as a calming influence and a cheerleader for the poetry community in general.

Scarlett admits that she struggles with the commonplace erasure of bisexual women in relationships with cisgender straight men; she feels that society is focused on the existing as opposed to the innate. To this end, she fights to represent bisexual writers and to reassure them that their lived experience is valid and important.

Juno Books
24 Chapel Walk
Sheffield
S1 2PD
0114 327 3426
hello@junobooks.co.uk
www.junobooks.co.uk

---

Book                                    £7.50

# Total.                                £7.50

Payment

Card:                                   £7.50

Thank you for your custom.
Please check our website for our
refund policy

---- VAT SUMMARY ----

Vat @ 20%.                              £0.00

---

Date      06-May-2023 15:22:21
Receipt   2,313

Book                          £7.50

**Total.**                    **£7.50**

Payment

Cash                          £7.50

Thank you for your custom.
Please check that items are for our full
refund policy

------ VAT SUMMARY ------

Vat A 20%                     £0.00

Date      06-08-2017 10:12:27
Assist... 2 218